B
POEMS A
BY

With the voices of my boys strewn in and
words for an angel

Copyright 2022 Rachael Hinkley

All rights reserved. No part of this book may be reproduced, stored in a retrieval system or transmitted in any form, or by any means, without the prior written permission of the author or publisher except by a reviewer who may quote brief passages to be printed in a newspaper, magazine or journal.

Cover Art by Vanessa Hogle. Photography by Rachael Hinkley. Graphic Art by Gwen Luckett. All rights reserved.

First Edition

First Printing

Published by Perfect Trust Productions

www.perfecttrustproductions.com

Dedication

FOR MY BOYS, MY LOVES, MY EVERYTHING. FOR MY HUSBAND WHO STOOD BY ME NO MATTER THE COST. FOR YOU, THE READER TO BE INSPIRED.

Foreword

I have known Rachael a very long time. I have watched her struggle and fight to become the amazing, strong, determined woman that she is today. Only through her tragedies could one fully understand her triumphs. In this book she gives you a peak of her heart and soul. A taste of what it's like to go through life battle scarred and proud. I couldn't be more proud to publish this book and watch her soar on the wings she has fought so hard for. It really is her time to fly.

Vanessa Hogle
Author
Publisher

SHOULD I

Should I stand or should I sit, doesn't matter the point is this.
Love thy neighbor was what we were taught, but destroy thy neighbor is how we were bought.

Displaying reckless character, name calling to the point of abuse, what's the use?
The days of structure and faith have all seemed to fade away.
Taken apart by misunderstanding, left alone due to notwithstanding.

Children running the street, unapologetic and rude to those they meet.
It's not a fault they claim, but the ones that gave them their name.
Afraid to set
them straight because society says they need a safe space.

Now we endure guns in the hands of the uneducated, mother's tears flood the gate.

Should I sit or should I stand?
I will stand, feet planted, and mind made up.
Teaching my kids to love thy neighbor, to lift thy neighbor.
Only through humility and grace will they ever find their true safe space.

Graphic art by Gwen Luckett (Reference to "Should I")

HOLD

Hold your babies close and tight, for those that are gone in the night.
Love them uncontrollably, for those lost at sea.
Teach them about their surroundings, some are too safe.
Show them how to navigate life, for some are too free.

Always keep them in your sights, even when they are grown
For some were never shown,
That there are monsters in the day and not just the night.
Teach them how to pull the trigger when they have the monsters in their sight.
Hold your babies tight, so as not to lose them to the night.

Photo by Rachael Hinkley

SOLDIER'S WIFE

She is scared, but she will never show it.
She is overwhelmed, but He will never know it.
She loves him unconditionally, so he will never doubt it.
She is dedicated to him, so he is proud of it.
She instills in him courage, so he will always have it.
She encourages him daily, so he doesn't succumb to it.
She endures restless nights without him but will never worry him.
She stays strong, for his weak moments.
She waits patiently for his return, never letting him see her cry.
She loves him intensely, so that he can endure.
She faces the days and nights alone but sends her comfort in a box to him.
Her face enlightens and her heart will skip a beat, when his boots are finally under her feet.
She is a soldier's wife.

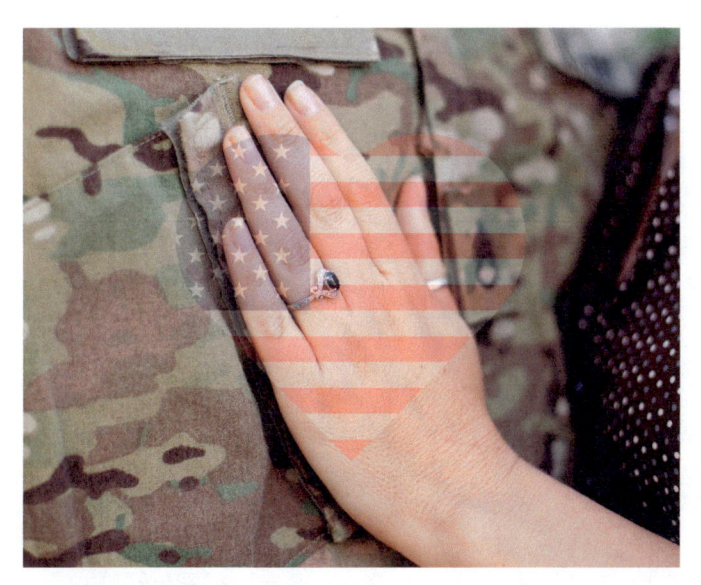

Graphic art by Gwen Luckett

FOR YOU

When I go silent, when I stop responding and you've done nothing wrong,
It's not because I don't want to talk to you, or that I don't love you, or that
I won't still ride or die for you.
It is because I am recalculating, reevaluating, resetting my mind, my spirit, my soul.

You see all of you get too heavy for me sometimes and going silent is the only option.

So that when the time comes, I can be at my best for you.
Respect the silence, let me be. If it, is you, I need to reset, I will tell you the truth,
Because there is nothing, I wouldn't do for me to do for you.

Photo by Rachael Hinkley

MY EYES

I've never seen through my eyes very clearly.
It's always been blurry and a bit hazy.
I've had to make my own reality and it's sometimes been chaotic and crazy.

I've taken for granted a life given to me,
but I've also been taken for granted that's clear to see.

I have pushed through the smoke and the blaze, hoping to see better days.
Only to find, ash still stirring and my eyes still blind.

Then one day a light peered in from the rear,
And for the first time, my eyes begin to clear.

I shielded my eyes from the light, for even that small amount was too bright.

Only to hear a voice tell me to look and not be afraid.
And when I lowered my hands, a soldier stood in my way.

He took me by the hand and kissed it gently.
I stood there in awe, trembling.

There was a shock the soared through me,
a feeling I didn't understand or even believe
How could someone so precious be sent for me.

He must have saw the question in my eyes and spoke

"God saw you couldn't see and asked whom shall I send and I said 'send me.'

He sent me to show you how beautiful you are, how special, and to let you know you're safe now, even in the dark. For HE only sends the greatest into battle the heaviest war.

So, take my hand and you'll soon see that through MY eyes, loved, safe, and happy you'll be."

Graphic art by Gwen Luckett

I AM

I am not your average cup of tea.
I am of the rarest breed.
I 've fought battles you can't imagine.
I come out battered and bruised every time.
I've seen things you can't unsee, heard things you wouldn't believe.
I've overcome the highest of mountains and withstood the lowest of valleys.

I realize now I need to shed this armor, lower my weapons, and sink to my knees.
I lift my eyes up to the heavenly skies, praying HE hears my cries.
I am NOT defeated, and I did not surrender. I simply need back up; I need a mighty defender.

For though I've walked through the valley of death, and I have feared no evil, I still need the comfort of the staff to do what comes last.

To let go of it all, to lay it all down
To get help straightening my crown
To be reminded of the moment he chose me
To remember I'd rather die on my feet that live on my knees.

Graphic art by Gwen Luckett (Reference to "I AM")

FOR MY BAMMY

There once was a girl who only wanted one thing in this world.
A boy for her to love
So, she looked to the heavens above
and prayed that God would send her a boy one day.

God smiled upon her as he heard her plea
And sent her not one, but three.

Then one day she realized that there was a spot in her heart for another one,
So, HE smiled again and gave her a grandson.

Graphic art by Gwen Luckett

CHAOTIC MIND

I want to run; I want to run!
This… what I am doing is no longer fun.
I sit alone, I eat alone, I sleep alone.

I stare at these four walls, slowly losing my mind.
All I want is peace I can't seem to find.

Restless nights
Anxious thoughts
A drink to help my mind rot
Take me for I am ready
Let's drive to levy
Park the car on the ledge
No one to hold my hand as I step off the ledge.

Let the water take control
Let it fill my lungs
For this, what I have been doing is no longer fun.

Photo by Rachael Hinkley (Reference to "Chaotic Mind")

BROKEN

I am broken
Laid up sullen
I cannot breathe for the pain
What is there now to gain.

All my efforts wasted
The good life never tasted
Is this what Hell is
Do people actually settle for this
My boys are all grown
My baby not reaping what he has sown
I am at my wits end
My heart and head won't mend

This mama is tired
Her ammo is all fired
The light's going
I don't know what I am doing

On my knees I look up
Through tear-soaked eyes, I give up
Lord take me now
Arms outstretched; head bowed
Take this pain from me
I'd give my soul to be free
For I am broken. Laid up sullen.

Graphic art by Gwen Luckett (Reference to "Broken")

ISAIAH'S WORDS

"I know you have seen things you wish you hadn't.
You have done things you wish you could take back.
And you wonder why you were thrown into the thick of it all.

Why you had to suffer the way you did.
And as you are sitting there alone, hurting…
I wish I could give you a shoulder and remind you that the world isn't all dark."

Photo by Rachael Hinkley

PRAYER

Prayer, a powerful notion of surrender, a wish to some, a livelihood for others.
A self-talk to a higher being, a one-way conversation with you only listening.
An uplift to heart and soul, a cursed adventure for the old.

A belief in something greater, a glimpse into the now and later
A sentiment on the wings of a whisper
A last-ditch effort to make a wrong right.

But what if what we deemed wrong, wasn't ours to rectify?

Graphic art by Gwen Luckett

QUIET

All is quiet in this house, the kind I like to hear.
I sit at this table listening to the wall clock tick in my ear.
I often get lost in its rhythmic sway, contemplating my day.
But this morning I sit and reflect on everything that I didn't regret.

These are troubling times, and the world seems out of sync
But I do not falter, nor overthink
I am simply reminded of times past, and how the bad never lasts
For the sun rises every day, even when storm clouds turn the skies gray.
All is quiet in this house, the kind I like to hear

Graphic art by Gwen Luckett

AWOKE for Mike 5/24/76-1/1/16

I awoke this morning with you on my mind.
I wondered why this time.
Did I have a dream, were you thinking of me?
I try to go back to sleep, but the notion eludes me.

I often hear your voice calling my name, and I awake to hear nothing of the same.
I feel the burn in my eyes as I begin to cry, wanting to hear your voice one more time.

As the year draws to an end, others wait for a new one to begin. I lay awake thinking of you and wonder if yours starts anew too?

I awoke this morning to the thought of you, I have to tell you this to make it true.
You're never really gone when your voice awakens me in a sweet song.

Photo by Rachael Hinkley (Reference to "AWOKE for Mike 5/24/76-1/1/16")

SISTER OF BROTHERS

I am a sister of brothers
I know first-hand the love filled tortures
I know the deepest love and strongest protections
I know the pain of broken dolls and the joy of getting to tag along.
But what I didn't know was that unconditional love never ends and that they were my best friends.

I never knew how strong the bond, until I lost one.
I love them like no others.
I am a sister of brothers.

Graphic art by Gwen Luckett

OLD MOTHER

Old Mother tell me the story of the ancient ones. Of loves lost and battles won.
Tell me a story of when things were bright and free.

Old Mother tell me of the days when wild ones roamed free, of when the Earth showed all her beauty.
Tell me of the conquests and raids, of the fair-haired maiden and their extravagant braids.

Of the warriors so gallant and brave, of the lands belonging to whom their flags raised.

Old Mother tell me a story of our people and all their glory.

Graphic art by Gwen Luckett

REFLECTION

Someone tell me what to do, tell me that what I feel isn't true.
Show me a better way, let me see tomorrow, today.
Take me to a place I long for, let me empty my head and get back to before.

Looking around there is no one I can see, no one to help me get back to me.
Turning I see someone looking back at me, showing me a glimpse of a better way.

The one looking back at me, is my reflection in the mirror showing me a glimpse of tomorrow, today.

Graphic art by Gwen Luckett

M.O.M

I am a mother of a Marine, and just like him, I am of the rarest breed.
I carried him in my person and held him to my chest.
I raised him to be good and he turned out to be one of the best.
He has his mother's love that knows no bounds,
Hurt him and I will unleash my hounds.

He will never lay his life down in vain, for a Marine in Valhalla she will gain
For there waiting on him, I will be,
holding the reins of all the motherfuckers my hounds put in chains.

My Marine is backed by his brothers and sisters in arms, this much is true, but they have nothing on his mother, or your soul should I have to come for you.
I am a Mother of a Marine, and just like him I am of the rarest breed.

Graphic art by Gwen Luckett (Reference to "M.O.M")

LOVE FOR A SOLDIER

As I watch him lace his boots, adorn his cover, and walk out the door,
I couldn't help but realize I loved him that much more.
From his goofy grin, to the dimple on his chin
From his soft touch to his unfailing love.

Knowing he is leaving me to help protect you should make me jealous, but sorrowful joy and pride is all I fare, that I have my own hero to share
My love for him is abundant as should yours be, because of his bravery, you and I live free.

So, as I lay awake tonight, you can sleep tight, knowing the love of my life is out there fighting on your side.

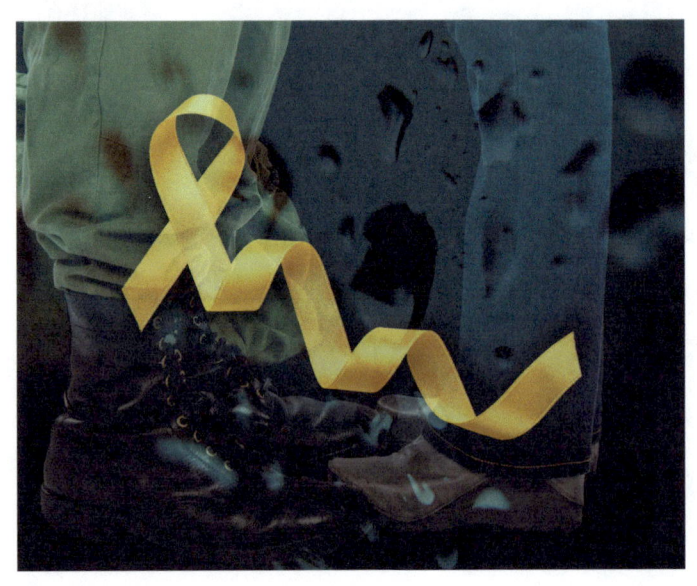

Graphic art by Gwen Luckett

MY LIFE by JALEN - first lyrics ever written that he threw away and I saved

All my life I felt no respect
When the times I hurt my brother, I felt regret
This poem is about my life and the people I hurt in my life

I wish I could delete those times, those negative thoughts
So, I could turn them into positive thoughts

When my life went wrong, my brother turned it to good

When my life went good my mother turned it to wood
Why wood?

Because wood is strong, just like my mom. So, this poem is about my life and of the people I gained respect in life.

Photo by Rachael Hinkley

THE ROSE by a very young Rae

What is it? It's a meaning of sweet innocent blood that perishes when broken or shattered by a slick silver. Sometimes it just sits there and welts.
Sometimes it weeps and withers.

But most of the time it stands together, then BANG!
Suddenly the rose turns black, weeps, and dies.

Graphic art by Gwen Luckett

WORDS FOR AN ANGEL by Deb Phillips auntie of an angel

This beautiful young lady, this vision you see, this is Rachael, a mother to be.
She was so happy, her dream had come true, her life was just right, she was pregnant with you.

She took care of herself; she really did glow.
She did everything so you'd properly grow.
But something went wrong, all her hopes were shattered
You weren't going to live and nothing else mattered.

Now mom is in pain, it shows in her eyes.
But that's what happens when a loved baby dies.
My heart breaks for her, I know what she'll miss.
Laughter and hugs and your first baby kiss.

No reading of stories and no Dr. Suess.
No counting your toes, no Old Mother Goose.
No singing of songs, no soft lullabies
But that's what happens when a loved baby dies.

No watching you sleep. No smelling sweet skin
Mom's arms are so empty her sweet baby girl dead
No seeing the world through new baby eyes
But that is what happens when a loved baby dies

In time the pain will heal, and she'll no longer cry.
But that's what happens when a loved baby dies
But God in his wisdom wanted you with him
Mom's sweet baby angel, her sweet Debra Ann.

The hurting will cease, the healing will start.
You're on our minds, always in our heart
The time has come to say our goodbyes, and this is what happens when a loved baby dies.

DEBRA ANN PHILLIPS 11/22/98-11/22/98

The above picture is a graphic design done by Gwen Luckett for Rachael Hinkley. This is not an actual depiction of the beloved child. The hand and footprints are from Debra's birth certificate and were added to the design to make it complete.

PSALM OF JAMES III by James Patterson III

Your chapter in my book is over, best not give it a second look.
I had walls and towers put up like they were rooks.
Often, I stayed up for hours reminiscing about the time that was ours.
I wanted to set a plan in motion and travel the ocean.
With you by my side, but darkness is where I will reside.
Your face is still plastered in my mind. It's all kind of redundant.
Now I am focusing on myself and becoming relevant.
All I speak is the truth, and this is a song to my youth.

I'm sorry if my words were lethal. Now it's nonresistant. They call me narcissistic,
Now they want to listen. So, pay attention. I never liked to claim anyone, it's all too foreign.

I wish no one pain, but it's a shame that life doesn't feel the same way.
All I speak is the truth, this is a song to my youth.
Thought it was a song about you?

Now I have a reason to be here and stay, I didn't know life could be this way.
Really came a long way with a knife in my back, believe me when I say nothing lacks.

So, all I speak is the truth, this is a song of my youth.

Photo by Rachael Hinkley (Reference to "PSALM OF JAMES III")

SOUTHERN SILENCE *a short story*

    Third pew from the front on the left, a quarter of the way in, that is where I would find her, where she always sat, no matter the church. For as long as I can remember, that is where she sat. In her best three-piece, Sunday best, adorned with a matching hat, pocketbook, and shoes, every Sunday morning, evening, Wednesday, and church event that didn't involve the outdoors. Third pew from the front on the left, a quarter of the way in is where I found her tonight. Sitting quietly and alone in the empty worship hall.
I know she heard the heavy door open as it echoed loudly in the empty chamber, and the rustle of my boots, my cuffs and keys clanking against my hip as I walked slowly towards her. I turned down my radio, so as to not disturb the quiet somber. I came to a stop next to her and watched her for a minute. Her head raised to the ceiling in silent contemplation, even in the darkened room, lit only by the soft spotlight above the crucifix behind the podium, I could see her eyes shut and a smile on her face, lips moving as silent words escaped into the abyss.
    I watched as her lips stopped moving, eyes still closed, she spoke, "Good evening Deputy."
I took a deep breath in and whispered my own silent prayer of strength and took up a seat behind her, to the right of her so I could see her face better. She never turned to look at me, never even budged an inch in any direction. She sat poised, determined, and steadfast. I patiently waited a few more minutes, looking beyond her at Jesus on the cross glowing in the soft light that surrounded him, "I haven't been here in years." I said softly. This made her turn her head sharply to the right, I could see the scowl on her face even at that angle.
In her deeply rooted southern voice, she spoke again, "Deputy, I am not surprised at that at all, however, there is no excuse for not gracing these pews."

I hung my head, took a deep breath, and swallowed hard before I spoke,

"No ma'me, there isn't, but I am sorry I did not come here to talk about my shortcomings in the church."

　　She turned and faced forward one more time. She sat so still and stoic, I was afraid to move, afraid to disturb the quiet. After what seemed like an eternity she slowly rose to her feet. Using the pew in front of her to steady herself, smoothing out her dress she placed her pocketbook under her right arm and bent to retrieve her hat.

"Grams," I said shakily, "you know you just can't walk out of here." She stepped out of the pew, turned, and faced me, looking down at me with her piercing blue eyes, pursed lips and elegant posture. I swallowed hard and dropped my head. Looking at my hands I began to fidget.

"I'm sorry Grams, I just meant…"

"I know what you mean Deputy," she cut me off abruptly. She took a deep breath, softened her tone before she spoke,

"Come child there is something I need to show you." With that she started back towards the door. I slowly rose and began to follow her. I watched her intently, I could hear my heart in my ears as she stopped at the door. She stood facing it and I saw a shudder in her shoulders before she straightened her back and turned to the left and put her hand on the basement door.

I swallowed hard and quickened my step. When I reached her I protested, 'Gram, no, I…"

"Hush now,' she warned

"Come, you're perfectly safe, I want to tell you a story."

　　She reached out her hands and I reluctantly took it. My feet felt glued to the floor as I tried to walk. I took her hand and she brought it to her lips and kissed it gently. She ushered me through the door. My heart was racing more and my palms began to sweat. Realizing this, she began to speak.

"You know my father built this church. My sister and I would play here while my father worked. Doing everything by hand, we didn't have the luxury of machines back then, just true blood, sweat and tears. That summer was a hot one and people were struggling for work, food and peace of mind. One day my sister and I were playing right out there, daddy had fixed a board to a rope and hung from that very oak tree there now and I was pushing Helen on the swing when a shadow cast over us. A shadow of a man. "
She paused a moment to look back at me as she led me through the fellowship hall, down the hall passed the Sunday schools. I swallowed harder, trying to figure out where she was going with this story. Even though I think, I already knew.

She stopped halfway down the hall and looked at a black and white photo of the church in its infancy. A group of men stood in front of it, and I watched as her gaze fixed on one in particular and her eyes went glossy. She shook her head, shut her eyes to stay off any tears that were surely welling up. She composed herself so eloquently before turning to me. That southern poise never faltered. She pursed her lips and let out a sort of snort through her nose, and begin again,
"The summer you and Kali came to visit grandpa and I. When you were twelve and Kali was eight, I knew something wasn't right. I saw an all too familiar look in your eyes. The same look that for an entire summer, stared back at me in the mirror. I tried to get you to tell me, and you just held it in so tightly that I began to see it become a part of you like an ivy to a building."
I felt my eyes go wide and my heart raced louder and harder, I could hear it pounding in my ears. I tried to pull away from her. She must have seen me go white because she grabbed me by the shoulders, looked me in my eyes and said, "Allison, look at me, you listen to me know you hear, we don't have much time, I need you to focus."
I took a deep breath and closed my eyes and nodded.

"That summer, I knew, and I talked to your daddy, I demanded that he tell me the truth and tell me what had been done to you. The way he looked at me, I knew! And my heart fell out of my chest. I was angry and disgusted and heartbroken that my own... my own son could be capable of such a thing."

I tried to pull away from her again and instinctively found my gun with my hand. Her hands slid down to mine and held it there on top of mine, gripping the latch of my holster.

"I begged him to leave you girls with me, your grandpa as well. They had such a falling out and, in the middle of the night, he took you both and we didn't see you again until you came when you were 19, Kali in toe and I saw the same look in her eyes."

She let that linger in the air as she pulled a chain she had around her neck, out of her shirt. A key was dangling from it.

"This key, this door," as she pointed behind her," holds a secret so loud, GOD himself has lost sleep. I stand here today, deputy, to tell you that I had the courage to break that silence and sacrifice my first born to save my last."

She held the key out to me and shakily I took it. She stepped to the side and motioned for me to open it. I slowly walked up to the door and my hands barely held the key. They were shaking so much. I turned the key and the door slowly creaked open. The first thing that hit me was the smell. The putrid smell of blood and excrement stung my eyes and my nose. I quickly brought my hand to my mouth and nose and covered them. I stepped through the dusty door frame into an all too familiar room. She walked in behind me and moved to the left of the room where a desk sat with a lamp. Turning on the lamp, it illuminated the room enough that I could see where the smell was coming from. There in the middle of the room was a blood-soaked mattress and a lifeless body lay upon it. Took me a minute to realize who it was, and the blood drained from my face.

Grams had sat herself in a chair that was sitting in front of the desk. She smacked her lips, took off her hat, and took a deep breath.

"Is he..." I begin

"No, he isn't. He is still my son after all, and as his mother it is MY responsibility to discipline him, even as an adult. You see, a mother always knows when her child does something wrong, needs correction or praise. As a mother, you never want to believe that your child could be capable of such atrocities. "
She shook her head, crossed her ankles and sat up straighter.

The body on the mattress stirred and groaned, moved enough that I could see he was anchored to the floor by a chain. His eyes fluttered open and once focused, went wide. He fixed on me, and his breath became fast and hard. He tried to speak but could not. His voice gone from the screams.
"You see child, he is just fine, a little wounded, but he will survive." She smoothed out her dress again and fidgeted with the cuff of her sleeve.
"I couldn't prove his misgivings, at least not until now. Until I came here to watch your sister get married and I saw the same look in the flower girl's eyes that I saw in yours and Kali's. That's when I decided that I was right. So, I began looking around. Being a nosey mom pays off and I have and always will be that mom. I found the key to this…" She waved her hand in the air. "This, this room, and one day I watched him take a sweet girl by the hand." her voice cracked and veered off.
"I heard the whispers, I watched as his sheep every Sunday flocked to his services. The ladies gossiping, turning a blind eye to what was happening to their own children! No one ever saying a word!" She yelled excitedly.

Composing herself one more time she softly spoke, "Until now. You see Deputy, Southern silence knows no bounds, a toxic cycle that needs cleansing. "
With that she reached under the chair and slid a box that her dress hid and placed it on her lap. She slowly stood, walked over to me, and handed it to me.
I looked from her to the box, to my father on the floor, and back to her again.

"It's okay sugar, I promise you he will not be hurting anyone anymore." She reassured.

With that she kissed my cheek, turned and walked towards a door on the opposite side of the room that led outside. She took a deep breath and repositioned her hat, stuck her pocketbook under her right arm and walked out into the night lit by the blue lights of patrol cars.

   My grandmother chained my daddy to the floor of that room four days earlier, beat him within an inch of his life with a four-braid willow branch. She told the court that she gave him a lash for every child's tear he caused. The number is still unknown. When she was finished, she made him pray with her and listened as he repented and when she was satisfied and convinced he was truthful, she called 911 and waited, in the 3rd pew from the front on the left, a quarter of the way in. The box she handed me contained enough of his sins to no longer be southern silence.

Photo by Rachael Hinkley (Reference to "Southern Silence")

SHE a short story

    To say she was easy is an understatement, borderline false. So defiant, on fire, independent, headstrong. She never gave in to being told no or that she couldn't do anything based on her gender. She'd just smile and say, 'watch me'. Sometimes she'd fall, but never down for too long, rising to do it right, better. She always got what she wanted, almost solely by her own hand. She came from nothing and rose to something. She never took a handout. She'd say she got that from her dad. She didn't really give much credit to her mom other than being grateful she gave her life, her beauty, and the one thing she said to her that stuck, 'never be afraid to speak your mind."
 When pressed on the issue, she'd shut down or become outraged, you never knew which as the outcome was unpredictable.
    Her only fear is the loss of her words, her voice is her power. Her babies are her life. Although I believe she is more afraid than what she will lead you to believe, the fortress she has built does not allow her to show it. Her strength, her resilience, is a work of art and I find myself in awe of her abilities. Many have tried to breach, and all have failed. Myself included and sometimes my patience wears thin, but I keep my distance and don't press the issue because of her innate ability to shut down and cut off. I watch and I listen, and I pray the love I have for her is enough. Sometimes she is difficult to love, and I find myself questioning my own strength in that endeavor, but I do love her or at least I try.
    I remember the first time I saw her, I was amazed at her beauty, her candor, and I didn't know if I could even measure up to such a beast. I had no idea at the time that her beauty came at a price so scarred and hid more than I even thought possible. I can't honestly say I would've fallen as hard as I did, had I seen the scars on that first day.

Each day after that first, I grew to know her, and slowly she started to show me her scars a little at a time. She wasn't aware of it at first, but one day she was a little quiet and when asked, *"I'm fine"* was the answer I got and that's when I began to see that wall. The encroachment of her fortress, she began to see as an invasion, and she would gear up for battle. I would get angry, blinded by nothing, not understanding her aggression. I didn't see how what I was doing was beginning to break her, and all she's known is to close up shop and not let anyone in. When I did see it, when I saw all the hurt, the pain, the abuse, she suffered at the hands of those who were supposed to love her, I saw it raw and untamed and I fought harder for her, to show her that I wouldn't do her that way. She would fight that much harder against me.

   I fought harder, mad at myself for being so selfish, so consumed by my own insecurities and demands that I was blinded by the fact that this magnificent beast before me was screaming for someone to help her heal. This incredible firebird was mine and I needed to protect her. I needed to be the one to tear through that fortress. I needed to stop being so selfish, so greedy… They say greed is the root of all evil, I say that the selfishness of a man towards a woman is.

I knew she was broken; I knew that her feet were covered in the ashes of those that burned her, and I saw that my own selfishness was sparking yet another fire. What I didn't know is that she would come back with a reinforced army no man could take down. In my weak mind, I shallowly thought, *'I got this, I can handle her,'* 'little did I know, I would be mistaken. One man should not be so naive to think he, alone, could tame such a creature.

Her fire, when lit, burns an inferno hell would reject. I loved that heat, loved that fire in her, even when it was me, she set ablaze. I craved it and I found myself adding fuel to her fire every chance I could. Burning up all the fire she had, good or bad, didn't matter. I was addicted and needed my fix. I needed it so much I didn't see it dying out. I didn't notice the embers fizzling out. Not until it was almost gone. I tried to reignite it, I tried everything I could to get her flame to burn bright again, but every spark I got was quickly extinguished by my own doing.

To say she was predictable, I would not bet on it. Just when you think you have her figured out; she throws in an audible. She never settles for yesterday, but sometimes chooses to settle for another day. Her battles are her own, leading them herself and running towards the sound of gunfire. Her bravery is something I can never match. I wish I could cut a piece of it from her, hold it in my hand, even if just for a moment. To bottle up this power, would be like trying to touch the sun.

She never shows weakness, never allows anyone to see her cry, and her anger is a force to be reckoned with should you ever provoke it. When her tears are seen, you get a glimpse of her darkness and when her fury is unleashed you feel the power of it.

To say she is beautiful is not a word I would use to describe her. She is not a beauty as you so conventionally know, nor does she try to be. I have seen beautiful women, and her beauty surpasses them all. She can't see what I see and often tells me she wished she could see through my eyes. I would gladly tear them out for her if it meant she could, even if only for a moment.

She's not your everyday girl, and that to me is why she is gorgeous. From her witty smile, her incredibly intelligent brain, her ridiculously ever-changing eyes, she doesn't lack in being gorgeous. She has flaws, but then again who doesn't. She cannot see past those, but I do. I may be the only one that can, for that, I cannot say.

My first instinct is to take away all her pain and darkness so she can see, but I can't. I can only tell her daily, show her every second in hopes that one day she will heal.

My selfish nature prohibits my recovery from her, and I reveille in the fact that I never will, nor do I want to. This fantastic beast, so wonderfully broken and chaotically amazingly made. I never want to be without her. I never want to give up what she possesses. I want to hold on to her beauty, her spirit and tame it. But something so exquisite, so exotic, cannot be caged. You can only hope to break the unbreakable. To tarnish something so resistant to blemishes, cannot be forged by any other means but her own. I learned to appreciate her chaotic beauty. Watching her makes her uncomfortable, she doesn't like it, but I can't help myself. I am in awe of every curve, every flaw, blemish, the way she moves, I get lost taking her all in. Fixated on the perfect storm of her.

To say she is anything but forgiving, may not be enough. She doesn't hold grudges; she holds the matches. She doesn't hold the hands that hit her, she doesn't initiate the fight. She will stand her ground, no matter the fate. She demands respect and more often than not she gets it. I wish I had her reservation and strength. Her forgiveness is not freely given, nor is her respect. Some sins include her own and those are harder demons to exorcize. Just because she forgives you doesn't mean she forgets. She would say that to forget would mean it never happened and that doesn't help to heal.

Some she has forgiven I think she shouldn't. She would tell me that what she does is never what anyone else would do and that her process is her own. God, I love her fire and tenacity. Love how she speaks her mind and isn't afraid to do so. She says to be afraid of your own mind or thoughts is like trying to cage a rabid dog. Forgiveness of herself is a different story, and I have seen in the years with her where she has slowly started to do that very thing. Watching her struggle with this is hard, but I cannot do this for her. This is hers alone to accomplish. I am here simply to help her when needed in this transition.

I have never seen a creature so vibrant and broken at the same time. She is truly astonishing to watch, a masterpiece that would have the greatest artist in awe of her. I wish I knew her full story, no one does. I am not convinced she even does, but that is a secret she will never reveal.

This amazing woman before me I can see the fire in her eyes and sometimes, I can see her demons, careful to not get too close. She says they're not for petting or feeding. I guess we all could take a page from her book. Take note of the fact that we are all quick to feed our own demons and wonder why they control our lives. Sometimes when I watch her sleep, I wonder if this is when she tames them.

To say she is anything but extraordinary is a waste of time. She is what we all should aspire to be. Beautifully broken put back together with gold. She has seen things you cannot unsee, felt things no one should ever feel. She has been holding the matches to the bridge you tried to cross when you shouldn't and through it all she has stood. Tall, unfolding, resilient. She has overcome where others would succumb. She will not submit, and I will not make her. But when she curls up in my arms and I feel her let go, just a little, I feel her more, I see her more and I love her more. She is a masterpiece, beautifully crafted by the fires that burned her.

Graphic art by Gwen Luckett (Reference to "SHE")

THOUGHTS

Leave me alone
Get out of my head, this is not your home
Leave me be
I rebuke you eternally
Take your bow and leave me now
Let me rest, this attention from you I detest.

Running, ravaging through my mind,
Has my stomach in a bind.
Making me unwell, can't you tell?

You seem to like what you're doing to me.
Creating chaos, never letting me sleep.

I expel you from my brain
I need to get off this train.

I ban you from my space
Leave now, never return to this place
Let me go back in time
When my thoughts were mine.

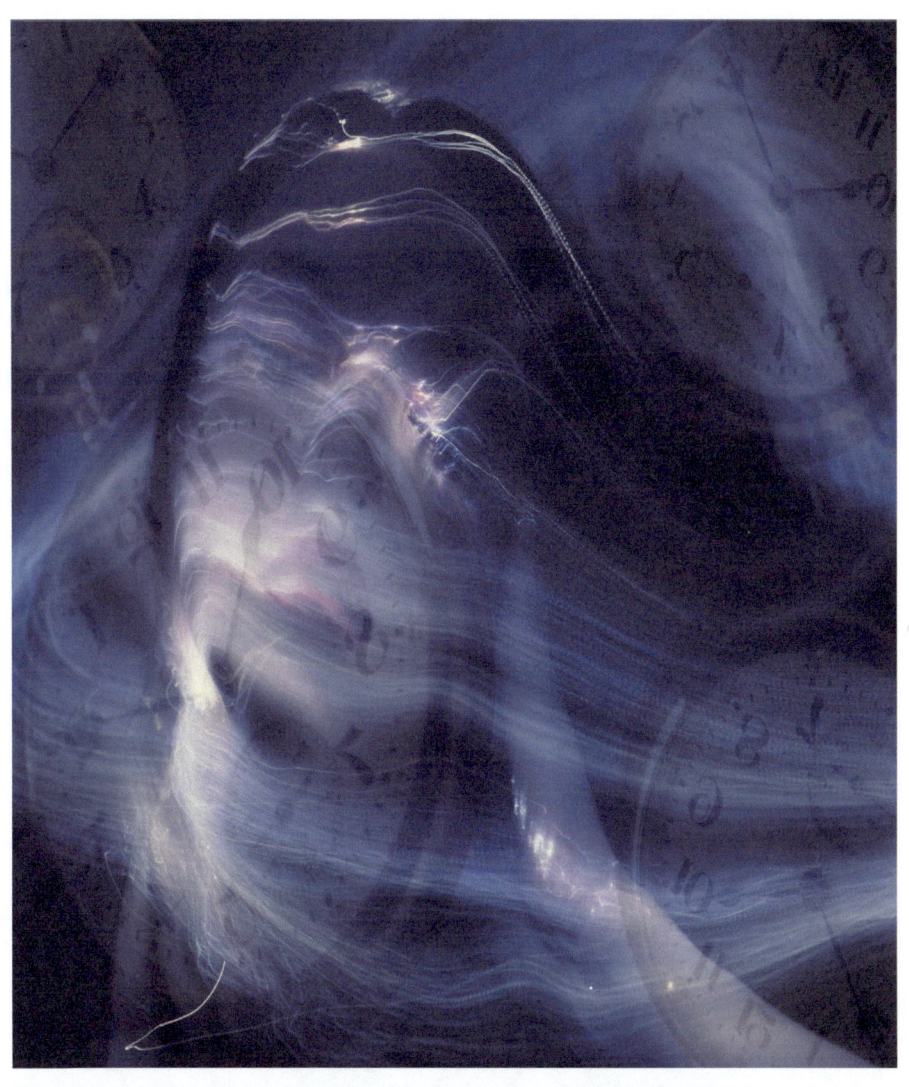

Graphic art by Gwen Luckett (Reference to "Thoughts")

MASTERPIECE *a short story*

    She watched him walk across the floor. Followed him with her eyes as she sat quietly in her chair. She dares not speak; she dares not move. He carefully and artistically placed her for his liking, and she dare not disturb that. She watched him pace, ever so often glancing over at her, only to shake his head, mumble and continue to pace. She timed her breath with his pace. In and out to the cadence of his footsteps. He promised he would be done soon. She did not know how much longer she would be able to hold the stature he placed her in. Her arms and wrists were beginning to ache, and her legs were shaking against the chair due to the cold. She took a deep breath to steady the trembles and took in the staunch of the basement, the musky cold air caused her to cough, which caused him to stop abruptly, and stare intensely at her. His nostrils flared and her heart skipped a beat.
    She could feel the blood pooling in her ears and let out a steamy breath. She met his eyes and watched him as he came closer to her. He stopped, inches from her, and cocked his head to one side, as if he were studying her. He pondered there a moment before he reached out his hand to grab the robe she had placed on the back of the lounge chair she was positioned on. His hand grazed her shoulder and she flinched. This gave him pause, if only for a second. He cannot let his emotions get the better of him. He needs to finish his work. He carefully draped the robe around her shoulders and leaned her forward to tuck it in the back. She moved fluidly with him, so careful to not disturb anything he has put into place. He gingerly set her back against the chair and covered her legs more with the thin sheet he had placed between them earlier.

He stood back, admiring what he had done, seemingly satisfied with his feat he nodded, and a sly smile creased his lips. She wanted to scream, she wanted to get up and cover herself completely and run out of that dreadful cold and damp basement, but she had a higher purpose, she had bigger things at stake here and she dared not entertain the idea of leaving anymore. She sensed he knew what she was thinking because the smile he dawned had begun to shift back into the puckered frown he so majestically wore. He turned and stormed back to his pacing spot. His pacing left a cleaned area on the floor, almost completely worn away the dust that covered the floor. He stopped in front of the canvas for a bit before picking up his paintbrush. He crossed his arms and tapped the tip of the handle against his chin, looked up at the ceiling, mumbled something before his brush strokes filled the air with rapid, harsh, uneven sounds reverberating off the walls of the basement.

Moving with such force and precision, no wonder some get lost in their movements and captivated by the hypnotic sounds the strokes made against the raw canvas.

He worked effortlessly for hours. Paint dripping on the floor, on his clothes, getting in his hair when he would wipe his brow. The robe had fallen to the floor and revealed her milky white exterior. She dared not complain about the cold, about the hunger she felt. She dared not move unless under his instruction. She caught herself dozing once, and his angry grunt startled her, and she regained focus. She did not know the time, the day, nor the hour. She knew she arrived on a Friday and the sunlight has not touched her skin since.

She fixated solely on his movements, on his cues, on his commands. She would endure no matter the time it took for him to complete his masterpiece she was determined to become. He told her there were others that graced the very chair she lays upon, and others he had shunned for one reason or another. They might have had the right look, but the wrong attitude or flare. He told her that the minute he saw her, he knew she was the one. She asked him once when was the first time he saw her, this answer, like him remains a mystery. The longer she was in that basement, the longer she looked at him, the more familiar he became, and she does not know if it is because it has been so long, or if she perhaps knows him from somewhere, someplace. Maybe in a different life they were lovers, she thinks. She also can't remember how she even came about to be in this murky room, or on this dusty lounge couch. Everything is a bit hazy. He promised he would be done soon.

Just as she was dozing off again, the sound of something dropping onto the floor startled her and her eyes fixed on the sound. Her eyes widened and her heart started racing, there on the floor he laid, eyes fixed on her, glossy and wide. She sat watching in horror, trying to understand what just happened. Comprehension eluded her faculties as she struggled to make sense of the scene before her. Panic started digging its nasty claws into her and her breath quickened. Struggling for ideas on what to do, she tried to move. She quickly realized she could not do that very thing. Was it because she had sat fixed in one position so long? She tried to move her arms and realized why they too were barely mobile. Her eyes shifted upwards and landed first on her wrist, bound with rope and suspended by a rope, her eyes followed upwards to a beam positioned purposely above the very place she sat. Horror followed panic in their pursuit of her faculties, and she tried to jerk her hands free and found they too weren't moving against her efforts.

Horror intensified its grip on her and she felt her breath becoming heavier, quicker, and suddenly she felt movement in her fingers, spiders crept down her veins as sensation came back to them. She turned her focus on her legs and tried to get the spiders to settle in her legs. Her feet moved first, painfully so, she cried out in agony. Realizing what she had done, her eyes darted towards him, and fear set in. Relief soon followed as she noticed he was still and no steam escaping his mouth, his eyes still fixed on her. She dared not take her eyes away, for fear told her not to. She slowly and painfully began to move one leg and then the other. She knew if she could stand, she could free her wrists from the beam. She placed on foot on the cold floor and then the other. The motion made her semi limp body fall forward and her shoulders burned against the resistance of the rope her wrists were bound to. She managed to stifle the cry of pain she felt. Her entire body was now on fire and waking as if for the very first time.

    She shakily stood to her feet, fearful of falling to her knees she was able to grab the beam and hold onto it for support. Once fully upright and as steady as she could manage, she studied the rope she was tied with as well as the beam she was tied to. Her eyes followed the beam and quickly realized to the left it was broken enough she could slip the rope through and at least free herself from the beam. She slowly moved to the left in a sideways slide motion, glancing from him to the beam and back again until she made it to the break. She had to tug a little to get the beam to break completely free, when it broke the sound reverberated against the walls and she immediately shot a look at the still man lying on the floor, fearful he would shoot up and attack her.

Suddenly flashes penetrated her mind and she realized how she came to be in this basement. Panic took over as she frantically searched the basement for anything to cut the ropes from her wrists, when her eyes landed on a painter's knife on a table behind the man on the floor. She slowly, cautiously moved towards him, stopping only because she thought she saw movement. Realizing he was still motionless, she quickly raced to the table, grabbed the knife, and awkwardly began sawing at the rope between her hands. Freeing herself she raced back over to the lounge chair, grabbed the robe and scanned the room for the door. Locating it, locked! Banging on it she started to cry, for she knew she would have to search the man for the key. Looking back over her shoulder at him, his eyes still fixed in the direction of the chair she was once in she turned and slowly walked back over to the man. Stopping to grab the sheet off the chair to throw over his eyes.

She quickly did so and hastily patted down the man's body. Her hand landed on the front pocket of his trousers, and she dug out a set of keys, a money clip and a cell phone. Relief set in and she rushed back over to the door, shakily trying every key until the right one slid into the lock and the glorious sound of it turning played musically in her ears. She shoved the heavy metal door open and it creaked loudly, the sunlight hitting her eyes like razor blades. She gave the door one last shove and she stepped out into the daylight and closed the door. She found a metal rod and slid it through the handles. She looked around for anything, anyone, any sign of life, that could help her. She looked down at the phone she had in her hands and quickly realized it was her phone.

Prayerfully she turned it on, hoping it would. Not realizing she was holding her breath, until it came out forcibly when the phone chimed to life. It started going crazy, beeping, and chiming with texts, notifications, and voicemails. The date on it read Thursday May 13. Her last message sent was Friday March 3. Even more horrified, she quickly dialed 911. Rescuers quickly came to her, as she sat in the back of the ambulance and the lights lit up the now dark sky, she oddly thought about the masterpiece. Surrounded by lights, paramedics and police officers, her attention turned to the investigators who brought it up out of the basement. She watched them load it into a van, covered with a painter's cloth, and she longed to see what was underneath.

Standing in her apartment, three months later, she holds a hot cup of coffee in her hand and her head is cocked to one side, admiring the masterpiece she once was.

Graphic art by Gwen Luckett (Reference to "Masterpiece")

BROWN EYED BOY

In your eyes I will always see that brown eyed boy staring back at me.
In your smile I will always feel your warmth surrounding me.
In your hugs I will take your embrace whenever I need.
In your hands you will always know the strength I've given you.
In your uniform I can see the man I always knew you'd be.
With your gear at your feet, I know my job is complete.
With tears in my eyes, I have never been so proud.

Please, my beautiful boy, don't ever doubt.
Take the God I showed you to love, know he will keep you safe from above.
Now pick up your gear and fall into place. Your time is now so wipe those tears from your face.

Just remember that no matter what, when you look at me, you'll always be that brown eyed boy staring back at me.
So, stand proud and stand free my United States Marine.

Graphic art by Gwen Luckett (Reference to "Brown Eyed Boy")

LETTERS TO MY SON

What do you say to a boy who you have carried in your womb for 9 months, cradled in your arms, held his hand to walk across the room, smiled at as he sleeps, when he tells you his dreams? How can you put into words how proud you are of his finger painting, or express how joyfully sad you are when he didn't need you to open his juice box? Where do you find the words to tell him when he drives out of the driveway for the first time on his own? How do you keep your mouth shut about his love life or the decisions he makes that turn into mistakes and lessons learned?

You just smile at him and hope that all the instruction, all the love, all the mistakes you made, pays off. You pray that God watches him as he ventures off, you take stock in the manners you instilled in him while he is in someone else's presence. Most of all you write him letters when he leaves.

Letters to my son to tell him how proud I am of him and hope he doesn't notice the tear stains on the paper. I write to tell him how everyone at home is rooting for his success and pray he doesn't read between the lines the sadness in my voice. I struggle to find the words to let him think we miss him without telling him to come home. I pray every time I pick up the pen and paper for God to guide my fingers to express encouragement, enlightenment, and pride.

Letters to my son give me something to look forward to while he is away, they allow me to tell him how much I love him without him seeing me cry. They allow me to remain his mom even though he doesn't need me anymore. They allow me to remain close when he is a thousand miles away.

Letters from my son allow me to shine with pride when I read them out loud to friends and families. They reassure me of my place in his life and remind me that no matter what, he is my son, and I am his mom and no amount of time and space will change that.

Letters from my son gives me relief that he is ok, answers my prayers of safety for him and allows me to sleep a little better that night. Each one a day closer to his return, each one a word away from him showing his own son one day the love a mother had for hers. Each sentence, a link in the chain, I thought was broken when he left.

Letters to my son to get him through the day, to make the time he spends away easier. Letters to let him envision that even though we love him, we still need him, but can do fine without him. Letters that he did notice the tear stains and did read between the lines, but prayers that his letters home I wouldn't notice the same.

Letters to my son are a superficial way to express love and admiration in a way I feel is never enough, but deep enough for him to have something to hold on to.

You see words to your son are never enough in a mother's eyes, but to a son they are everything. From the subliminal ``I miss you' he got from the "we are so proud" and the "don't quit', to the tear stains he traces with his fingers.

Letters to my son take the sting out just a little, but letters from my son make it all worth it. They are stepping stones that lead to the day he walks back through my door, and I see a man in the spot where my son used to be. In all that he is and that smile he gives when he is in trouble, and a shoebox full of the letters I wrote to him in it.

Graphic art by Gwen Luckett

DADDY

The highway was empty aside from the occasional tractor trailer on their overnight hauls, she had rolled the window down to smoke a cigarette. Leaning on the windowsill she felt the cool summer breeze rustle her hair and blow the smoke back into her face. She did not notice that it stung her eyes. She was fixed on the road, on autopilot and her mind wandering back to the time she had last been to this place she found herself on this open haunted highway back to. It had been 23 years since she last graced the steps of that wraparound porch. How she loved to sit in the porch swing on summer nights, with a book and cool glass of sweet tea, how her bare feet tiptoed out of the screened in door, careful to avoid the creaky planks daddy swore he'd fix one day, how that last summer she did not care if her feet brought to life those old boards. How that summer that porch saw more than it had ever bargained for. She had replayed that hot August day over and over again in her mind, just a constant repeating scenario her mind couldn't turn off. The tears stinging her cheeks and the smoke making them burn even more. She cared not.

Her mind drifted to the phone call she received not 12 hours previous and heard the desperation in her mama's voice as she struggled to talk. She only managed to say, *"come home,"* before she hung up. She remembers standing at the kitchen counter holding the phone to her ears as if her mom would just speak again, despite the fact the dial tone rang in her ears. The busy signal prompted her to put it back on the receiver. She turned to see her husband standing in the door frame, leaning on the threshold, arms folded across his chest, eyebrows furrowed into a concerned look. She spoke only one word, *"daddy."*

Suddenly she was thrust back to 23 years prior and the voices echoed in her head, the smell of the air flushed through her nose as if just now smelling it for the first time. The honeysuckle so ripe, mama's pies cooling on the counter, daddy's pipe lit and smoke filling his study of a sweet aroma she loved to smell, and the smell of the steam in the bathroom as she sat staring at the two pink lines willing one of them to fade away. She sat there mesmerized at the sight of those lines, a million things running through her head. Footsteps down the hallway, the bathroom knob turning and the door opening, her name being called, broke her trance as she turned to see her mother standing in the doorway questioning if she had heard her calls.

Terror froze her as she watched the smile fade from her mother's face. Her mom quickly looked behind her and closed the door. She did not say a word, she only walked over to her and held her in her arms, silently taking the very thing she was so fixated on. *"It's going to be ok honey; we will fix this."* is all she said to her as she kissed her head. She looked up at her mama and tears dripped on her face. Her mama quickly wiped them away and tucked the two pink lines into her apron pocket. As she turned to leave, she grabbed her mama's hand and asked*," are you going to tell daddy?"*

She patted her hand, smiled, shook her head, and said*," no baby,"* a sigh of relief was short-lived when she finished, *"you are."* and left the bathroom and herself to her thoughts. Panic exploded in her like a summer drought fire through a wheat field. How the hell was she going to do that. Only last week she had excitedly told him she had been accepted to his Alma Mater school and the look in his eyes of pure pride and admiration for his only child. His baby girl was now going to have a baby herself. She sat in the bathroom for what felt like an eternity before she gathered up enough courage to walk the 20 steps from the bathroom to his study.

Reaching the door to his study she paused, closed her eyes and said a prayer. Turning the doorknob, listening to the hinges creak sent shivers down her spine, she shakily called, *"daddy?"* He looked up from his book and placed his pipe on its stand, he always gave her his full attention. Her eyes began to burn with hot tears she could feel burning her cheeks, her heart pounding. Seeing this he motioned for her to come to him and sit with him on the couch. She did not want to do this, but a hand on her back gave a little shove. She didn't notice her mama was behind her. She slowly walked over to her daddy and sat cautiously beside him. Her mama stepped just inside the door and waited anxiously for a moment before reaching into her apron pocket, closing her eyes and walked over to the desk, she slowly laid the two pink lines on its glossy surface.

He never said a word, he only looked at the stick on his desk, looked up at her mama. Standing to his feet, she reached for his hand, and he violently jerked away. He shot her a glaring look, one she had never seen before, one that sent a chilling fire to her very core. The room erupted into chaos, he picked up the test, yelled obscenities at her, to her, to her mama, to God. Wandering how this could happen, how she could let this happen. How now she was tainted, ruined, disgrace, and has thrown her life to shit. Her mother desperately tried to calm him, and he refuted her advances and accused her of coddling the girl too much.

She sat on the couch crying into her hands, he had taken her by her shoulders and pulled her violently up towards him and shook her angrily. Her mother furiously stepped in between, she broke loose, and she ran, she ran not knowing where she would go, what she would do. Not noticing the screen door, she tore through, not minding the creaking floor boards, not even noticing him standing there in the driveway as he caught her in his arms. She fought him a moment before she realized who was holding her and she cried hysterically into his arms.

The cocking of the gun made her turn sharply around as her daddy came barreling down the steps forging a 30-gauge shotgun. He shoved her behind him and valiantly approached her daddy and met the shot gun at its tip. She ran to stand in between him and the gun. *"NO!"* she yelled at her daddy. Her daddy stood there, gun raised at her instead, he did not waver. He stood defiant against her, not hearing the pleas of her mother.
   He swallowed hard and lowered the shotgun. He stood enormously over her, looking over her head at him and coldly, angrily, spoke, *"Go, take her, and don't bring her back."* With that he left them in the driveway and ordered her mother back into the house. She refused him and ran out to her, hugged her and placed a wad of cash in her pocket. *"Go love, he will calm down, but for now go."* Her mother whispered in her ear as she held her close.
   23 years later, she is barreling down the same road, turning onto the same half mile dirt driveway, still hearing the gravel flying behind his beat-up pickup truck as it had clanked against her SUV. 23 years later, she came to a stop in the very spot he had shunned her.
   The sun had begun to break over the house and bring to life a new day. She sat in the car and closed her eyes and welcomed the birds chirping in her ears and allowed the sun to gently warm her face through the windshield. She heard the screen door creak open and heard the familiar sound of the floorboards creaking as she walked down the steps and heard her shuffled walk approach her car. She did not open her eyes until she tapped on the side of the car. She slowly opened her eyes and sat looking out the windshield, afraid to look at her, afraid to see her in her pain. "Come child, he has been asking for you all night." She said and opened her car door.

She swallowed hard and squeezed the tears back one more time, and slowly got out of the car. She followed her mama into the house and was greeted by the same sweet smells she once loved. She passed the double doors to his study and noticed they were opened; something caught her eye and she paused and walked in. Her mother quietly fell in behind her. She walked into the musty room, stale with cigar smoke. What caught her eye was a photo hanging high on the wall behind his desk chair. It was of her, in her cap and gown as she graduated Cum Laude from his Alma Mater school. It was a newspaper photo he had enlarged and framed. She slowly looked around the study and was greeted with an array of photos and newspaper clipping, her eyes stopping on a picture frame on his desk of a rosy cheeked baby girl and his own eyes staring back at him.

She picked it up and looked up at her mama. She was standing in the door frame, with her hands in her apron pockets and her lips fixed in a loving, pursed sort of way. She smiled and nodded. A simple, eloquent nod. Turned and walked out of the doorway and up the steps. She followed behind her as they headed towards the very room, he laid waiting for her. She was greeted with the sound of machines pumping and beeping and the smell of antiseptic stung her nose. Her daddy laid in a hospital bed covered in tubes and wires. Her mama had gone over to his bedside and grabbed the remote to the bed to raise the head of it. His eyes slowly rose to meet hers and tears were streaming down his face. Her mama gently wiped them from his eyes and kissed his cheek. She turned to her and nodded that same nod again as she walked over to her, kissed her cheek, and walked out of the room.

She stood there for a moment, afraid to move. It was he who spoke first in a hoarse, scratchy voice, "Come,' is all he said and she slowly made her way over to the bed. He held up the fingers of his right hand and so tragically tried to raise his hand. She took it in hers and brought it to her cheek, he stoked it gently with his index finger. Tears crept down her face, she just held his hand there and sank to the chair her mama had positioned there before she left. She just sat there holding his hand to her cheek, crying uncontrollably. He shushed her, she looked up at him and met his eyes. The very same eyes she had looked at for 23 years in her own daughter, the same eyes he had looked at for 18 years and hadn't seen for 23. He just sat there looking at her, looking back at him. Nothing was said, nothing needed to be said. All that was, was and all that is, is right now. In that moment, all was forgotten and forgiven.

    His left hand was stronger than his right and he pointed towards the dresser that sat across the room from the bed. She followed the gaze and realized he was pointing at a wooden box. She let go of his hand and walked over to retrieve it. She noticed it was hand carved and engraved with initials, her baby girl's initials, and the tears flowed again. She brushed over the initials with her fingertips, before lifting the lid. In it was a letter addressed to her daughter and a lock of hair that she recognized to be hers, along with photos of her as a baby and of her holding her baby.

She closed the box and held it to her chest, turned and walked back over to where her daddy laid silently watching her. She stood looking at him, meeting his gaze again, she nodded. He let out a sigh and tears flooded his cheeks again as he closed his eyes and seemed to relax. She took a tissue and wiped his cheeks, kissed his head, and laid her head on his chest. She laid there listening to the beeping of the machines as he laid his left hand on her hand and stroked her hair. She laid there, tears soaking his pajamas, she laid there. She laid there until his hand fell limp against her head, she laid there as her daddy peacefully faded away. She laid there as her mama turned off the alarm on the machines, she laid there, forgiven, loved, renewed, heartbroken. She laid there, with daddy.

Graphic art by Gwen Luckett

WIND

Cool summer breeze,
Wind whistling through the trees,
Bare feet in the grass,
Vibrations from the Gods telling stories of the past.

Electric currents running through my veins,
God of wind holding the reins,
His soft touch encompassing me
Taking control of my senses completely.

The air that fills my lungs grab hold of my chest
Caressing my being, swelling my breast.
Zephyrus invading my soul
Bringing new into the old

Breathing him in effortlessly
Welcoming him majestically
Taking in all his healing powers
Getting lost in the hours

Each breath is sweeter than the last
Exhaling all my unwanted past
Putting me back together so seductively
Erasing all the trauma that tried to kill me.

Photo by Rachael Hinkley (Reference to "Wind")

FOREVER

Never say forever, for it isn't real
It isn't something lasting, it's what you think you feel,
So, if you tell me forever, please say you'll try
Because sometimes forever means goodbye.

Graphic art by Gwen Luckett

Mother's Justice

Water dripping, clinking against the stainless steel of the sink. Echoing off the barren walls. The damp, moldy smell filling his lungs. Coughing, he slowly opens his eyes. Pain immediately reverberates through his body. Blinking against the dark he tries to orient himself. Cloudy memory of the night before seeps into existence. He struggles to move and finds himself bound. By what, he cannot tell. His limbs have gone numb below the elbows and knees. He tries to speak and finds his words silenced by what he assumes is duct tape covering his mouth. Making it even more difficult to breathe. He looks around, trying to get some sort of idea on what the hell and where the hell he is. He grunts against his restraints in an effort to move, even just a little to relieve some of the pressure. The dripping of the water sound amplifies in his head, and he is greeted with white lightning pain that causes him to close his eyes and breathe deep through his nose. The familiar smell of pennies mixes with the mold in his nostrils, as he realizes the predicament, he is in.

Somewhere from behind him a loud, metal against concrete sound followed by creaking, a light floods in. Illuminating his shadow in front of him. Footsteps replace the leaking faucet as they echoed throughout, inching closer, one slow, methodical step at a time. Humming cadenced the footsteps as he recognized the sound stilettos make against a concrete floor. Not just any stilettos, 7-inch Prada, that adorned well-manicured toes and legs leading up to the devil's lair. A very eloquent, blood red manicured finger creased up his back, around his shoulders and stroked his face. He violently tried to tear away from the talons of evil incarnate.

"Oh, why so angry, pet?' she asks in her seductive voice. Flashbacks of the night before shown in his head like a broken movie reel, he quickly pieced together how he came to be her captive instead of her captor. He somewhat knew she would not be so trusting the minute he saw her, but something about her intrigued him. He had never seen someone so captivating, at that age. He thought, *'man here comes trouble.'*

She didn't want his advice, nor his expertise. She wanted more; she wanted his balls in a vice around her neck. Through countless pursuits, he settled on at the very least fucking the hell out of her, or at least he tried. Comes to find out, the Devil's mistress cannot be exorcized through dominated sex. But the efforts did not come without a price. Once he realized the demon under the makeover facade, he cut his ties. He left, she didn't take too kindly to that notion and began her brutal pursuit that made fatal attraction look enticing.

Restraining orders, court appearances, and even a prison stint, did not sway this beast when it came to what she deemed hers. He thought he had cured himself of her possession. Though he exhausted the very essence of her, until last night.

He watched her as she glided by him and stood in front of him. His eyes cut razor sharp glares at her, visualizing the very moment he would attack. She folded her arms across her chest, cocked her head to one side and laughed. Her piercing shrieks echoed off the walls in an endless bounce of raw, unadulterated, sinister, callousness.
"Oh pet, if looks could kill, I would be dead right now." she chuckled.

She slowly walked over to him, put her hands on his arms and dug her nails into wounds he didn't even realize he had; lowered her top half of her body to him, face to face.
"But it looks like the devil protects me even still." and she kissed the duct tape covering his mouth. He tried to move away, all he could do was snort violently at her, frowning in disgust.

She stood, took her right hand, and stroked his cheek, grabbing the tape by one corner, tearing it from his face, taking some facial hair with it. He yelled out in pain, "BITCH!"

"Uh uh uh, manners pet. No need for such language." she warned
"What the fuck did you do?" he questioned angrily

She didn't answer right away. She stood straighter, stroked her hair, and walked over to the left of him and retrieved another chair that had been sitting in a dark corner.

She sat the chair directly in front of him, carefully stepping over something in the floor, waved her hand absently in the air. A switch clicked somewhere behind him, and he realized they weren't alone. The crackling of fluorescent light came to life and the room illuminated. Blinking against the light he struggled to gain clear eyesight. She sat there a moment, giving him a minute to collect himself and see what awaited him to see.

"I did not do anything my pet, you did." she answered flatly, almost angrily. She was always so poised, so eloquent, never to allow anyone to see her vulnerable, even through anger.

He looked around the room, concrete walls, floors and ceiling. By the sound of it a steel reinforced door. A butcher's sink in the corner with the leaky faucet. A mop and bucket perched next to it. A cot, a small wooden table to the left of him where she had retrieved the chair, a stack of books on the table and papers strewn across the cot. His field of vision traced a deep colored stain on the floor to the center of the room where it landed in a pool under a body. His eyes went wide in horror, and he sucked in air. There, face up, positioned haphazardly between her and him was a body, a female body, one he definitely recognized. His wife.

"WHAT THE FUCK, I WILL KILL YOU!" He shouted as he violently thrashed in the chair he was strapped to.
"I WILL FUCKING KILL YOU AND FEED YOU TO MY DOGS!" Infuriated, she leapt to her feet, jumped over the body and punched him in his nose
"You sir will watch how you talk to me!" she warned.
Blood filled his mouth and throat, and the cracking of his nose told him it was broken. Looking at her hand, she smacked her lips and said," I should kill you now for making me break a nail."

"I will do more than that when I get out of this chair you crazy ass bitch!" He said through gritted teeth.

She looked at him, pondered on hitting him again, decided against that and walked back over to her chair and positioned herself back in it. Poised there like a crow on a barren tree limb, she started to speak again,' let me tell you a story. One of trifling heartache, shame, grief, and revenge. One that will make you reconsider if not choke on your own words. You see when I first met you, you knew me not, but I knew you. Oh, I knew you well. I was afraid to approach you the first time, afraid you would recognize me. However, when I got the courage to approach you that fateful morning, I knew instantly that you did not, in fact, know who I was.'

He cocked his head to one side, rummaging through memories and keynotes in his life, and could not place her aside from that initial meeting. Seeing the quizzical look on his face, she smiled and decided to give him a clue.

"My name isn't what I told you it was, well the first name is true, but the last is Harris and not Calhoun. Naomi Anne Harris to be exact" She told him

She let that sink in a moment, smiling as she watched recognition turned his face white with horror.

"Mother to Cassidy Marie Harris. Cassie was what her father and I liked to call her. She was such a sweet baby. A true miracle she was. I had lost three before her, and when we got pregnant with her, we were overjoyed yet cautious. I quit working and focused solely on the precious gift growing inside me. Premature by only a month, and yet she was a fighter, a true fighter. She grew to such a loving, free spirited young lady. So full of life, so carefree. Afraid of nothing, absolutely nothing."

He realized his mouth was gaping open, he closed his mouth and swallowed hard, the taste of pennies burning his throat. The very mention of her name sent an electrifying chill down his back. He stiffened his back and hardened his face, sucked in bloody spit through his nose and hawked it on the floor, landing close to the lifeless body of his wife.

"Classy, a real gentleman you are." She said condescendingly as she stood and walked over to the cot, retrieved the papers that were strewn about, before she walked back over to where he sat. He watched her every move, as much as he could at least.

Clearing his throat, he barked, "Fuck you, I didn't do anything to her that she didn't want."

She paused, closed her eyes, took a few deep breaths in, and backhanded him. Causing his head to snap viciously to one side, blood spraying out of his mouth, spitting it onto the floor.

 She took his face in one hand and shoved a photo of a young naked, mutilated, bloodied, girl in his face, yelling, "IS THIS NOTHING YOU FUCKING ANIMAL!??' Forcing the photo into his mouth. He tried to spit it out, but she kept shoving it in his mouth until his teeth scraped her knuckles. Satisfied that it was all in there she stood, wiped her bloodied hand on his shirt, turned and sat back down in her chair. He struggled to get the photo out of his mouth but managed to spit it out where it came to rest on his chest.

"I was making her favorite dinner that night, she had asked me that day before school if I would. So that day I went to the store, got all the ingredients to make chicken enchilada casserole. I even picked up a movie she had been wanting to watch. She would always laugh at me for 'renting' movies, calling me old fashioned, but then she would curl up next to me on the couch and watch it. Became our Friday night routine. That evening as I prepared the very dinner she asked for, I heard the garage door open and close. I listened for the sound of her voice chiming at the ring doorbell,' hey mom!' What I got instead was feedback from, what I now know was, the officer's body radio and my husband's muffled voice asking over and over again, *'are you sure?'*

She choked back her tears, closed her eyes and collected herself. *'this fucking animal didn't deserve the satisfaction.'* she thought.
Clearing her throat, she continued. "The rest was all a blur; I don't remember much at that point. Not the ride to the coroner's office or the questions from the police. The only thing that I absolutely cannot EVER get out of my mind is seeing my precious, sweet, 13-year-old baby girl, laying all alone on that cold slab. Only her head showing for identification. I later found out the real reason they did not uncover her body and why she would later only have a closed casket service."

She rummaged through the photos and papers she had in her lap, stood up and began tossing one by one on to the body that laid on the floor, circling it before stopping once again in front of him
"You see, my daughter met a monster disguised as a coach, a mentor, a trusted adult she came to admire. One she talked about relentlessly. Not knowing that this coach, this monster was married to someone even Satan himself would not claim. Now at first, I did not blame this monster, no sir I did not. I gave it the benefit of the same doubt you give a stray dog. She looked helpless, pathetic even, as I watched her with those other girls. It wasn't until I saw her special attention focused on a girl, one that oddly resembled my Cassie, that my grief turned to horror!'
She stood there a moment, allowing him time to reflect on what she had just said.

"Look lady, I did my time, paid the price." She hit him again before he could utter another word.
"TIME! You think a measly 10 years is enough TIME! Try a fucking life sentence, because that is what you gave my daughter! My husband and I! TIME!? "She viciously yelled, spit spraying out of her mouth like a rabid dog. She quickly regained her composure. Disgusted, he thought he would try his luck with whoever was behind him.
"Hey buddy!" He called behind him." Hey, are you just going to stand back there and let this crazy bitch get away with this!? This is kidnapping, assault..." Another blow to nose stunned him, snapping his head back against the chair

"Oh pet, you have no friends here." with that she looked up and motioned for whoever was behind him to come.

"You see, pet, I knew that for someone like you, that my daughter wasn't your first. No, no she wasn't. So, you know what I have been doing these past 10 years you were getting three hots and cot in the state pen??? Hmm? I was researching you, love. And well just let me show you what I have found."

She motioned for the person behind him to come closer, assuring them that it was ok, and to not be afraid. The creature from the dark shuffled cowardly and timidly towards her, head lowered so her hair hid her face from him. She stood in front of Naomi, back to him. Naomi smiled and brushed her hair out her face. Revealing a gruesome scar that permanently marked the left side of her face from her eyebrow, cut through her left eye, to top of her lip. A scar that left her without the use of her left eye.

"There now, that's better." Naomi reassured her.

"You see, I knew someone like you did the things you did to my daughter before. Yes sir, and I found one you forgot to make sure she was dead. One, as a mother, I know why you left her alive. One that will put an end to your tyrannical, sadistic, reign on young girls. '

With that, she lifted the chin of the girl before her, kissed her cheek, and walked around her. Stopping at the monster she had tied to the chair. He looked up at her, flinched as she raised her hand to his cheek. Stroked it and walked out of the room. The girl stood still with her back to him, staring at the back of the room. She felt her eyes sting and fill to the brim with wet hot tears. She methodically bent at the knees and patted the blood-soaked shirt of the woman lying on the floor. She closed her eyes and retrieved the 38 special revolver that was placed there under the dead woman's shirt. Slowly rose to her feet, held the gun to her chest, took a deep breath and slowly turned around to face the monster that left her for dead 15 years earlier.

He watched her turn slowly towards him, arms already locked, and finger positioned just above the trigger. His eyes fell on the gun first, following the barrel, to the hand that held it, to the arms stretched out bracing it, to the sight locked on his head landing on the face aiming it.

His heart stopped! He felt the blood drain from his face. He tried to speak, but no words came. He could not believe what he was seeing before him. She saw the look in his eyes and hesitated, "Abby, baby girl..." he cautiously started, was all it took to snap her back from the hesitation and pull the trigger. The gun echoed through the chamber, screaming at the walls. Connecting with his head, permanently fixing his mouth open, his last words still lingering in the air. She lowered the gun, letting it fall to the ground. She stood there, but only for a moment. For a moment she felt sad, but a wave of relief overpowered the sadness. She took a deep breath, collected the gun, the shell casing, the photos off the body and placed the chair Naomi had been sitting in back next to the table. Satisfied with the room, she walked over to where he sat, forever silenced, head slumped back, she kissed his cheek.

"Goodbye daddy, may you rot in hell." She whispered in his ear.

She walked over to the steel door, walking through it she struck the match against its threshold and threw it over her shoulder. She heard the whoosh of flames engorge the chamber and felt the heat as she closed the door behind her. Naomi waited for her just outside the steel door, watching as smoke sifted up into the night sky.

"Thank you, Naomi, thank you for everything." She said as she walked over to Naomi

Naomi smiled, took her face in her hands and kissed her cheek. "You're so very welcome sweet girl, they won't hurt anyone else anymore. I am so proud of you."

As they got into their own cars, each looking back at the entrance to the bunker. They left their monsters in to burn in the hell they created. Each turning their cars in different directions, to different yet very familiar lives. That night she laid in bed next to her husband, and for the first time in years she slept. Soundly, restfully, peacefully, slept.

Graphic art by Gwen Luckett (Reference to "Mother's Justice")

WORDS

Have you ever seen electricity flow from someone as they speak?
See it raise roofs and bring others to their feet.

Hear the magnitude of their power ring in your ears,
Sit captivated, brought to tears

Listen as if they're speaking only to you,
Resonating on the words you deem to be true.

What about words unspoken
Silence that rests on the tongues of the broken

Silence that shatters walls and breaks hearts
Silence that cut deep and leave a tale of scars

So powerful and majestic
So profound and authentic

Have you ever seen someone scream so loud, but never utter a sound?
Hear voiceless cries echoing so profound

Words are powerful this much is true
But we must give silence the respect it is due

Graphic art by Gwen Luckett (Reference to "Words")

SELENOPHILE

When asked why I love the Moon,
I just smile with pure delight

The answer is simple
The Moon is the ultimate light.

Its magic knows no bounds.
Its cycles move the waters that shake the grounds

Forever illuminated
No matter the time of day

Shines for the world to see
It brings forth all we seek

I love the moon for it triggers the night
And brings my darkness to light.

Photo by Rachael Hinkley (Reference to "SELENOPHILE")

ME

If I am me, then who are you?
If what I see is me, then who is it that looks back at me?
If the person I am is that of you,
Then are you the person in me that is true?

I do not know who I see.
Could it be you or could it be me?
Is there a reason, possibly?
For the you I see?

Changes I miraculously make
Mirrors I no longer break
Who is this I see, but in fact a new me.
Chaotically, beautifully, me
 is who I see.

Graphic art by Gwen Luckett

A SISTER'S LOVE- short story inspired by my honey bear's dream

   I was four years old when my sister died. I know that seems young to remember that far back, but that memory I will forever hold with me. I will carry it with me always. It was a warm summer night and my parents wanted to have a nice evening alone to celebrate a new chapter in their lives. They had just purchased their very own home, one that was equipped with state of the art everything including an enormous backyard that butted up against a thick, luscious, green forest. There was a fence around the property, but the trees, vines and shrubbery made it almost impossible to see it. My dad vowed to make the chain link fence a tall wooden privacy fence, but he never did.
  That night was like any other , my oldest sister, who was 12 at the time, had been in charge of me before and she loved the time she got to spend with me and never complained about having to be on brother duty, so when our parents asked if she would in fact, do that very thing this hot August evening, she accepted with delight.
  After the goodbyes and the abundance of kisses we were left to our own vices of each other's company. I don't remember exactly all the events of the night. I am sure we did all sorts of things like coloring, legos, etc. The biggest thing that I remember very clearly is the treehouse we discovered in the very back left corner of the backyard. It was overgrown with tree limbs and ivy. The rope ladder was still in good climbing condition, but my sister insisted she go up first to make sure the rest of the tree house was secure.

The ivy and brush were so thick that my sister could not break away the entangled greenery. She instructed me to wait there, as she ran to the garage and retrieved the hedge trimmers. The garage was in the front of the house and accessible via the kitchen. I promised I would stay put as she ran back towards the house and disappeared through the sliding glass door that led from the patio into the mudroom and into the kitchen. I watched her disappear into the house and turned my attention to the treehouse. I remember it seemed so big to my small stature and very intimidating to look at, ominous even. I remember standing there tracing an ivy from the base of the tree up towards the treehouse and losing it in the tangles of the ivy when a noise caught my attention. Thinking it was my sister I turned back towards the house to be greeted with nothing.

I heard the sound again and well, being a curious boy, I followed it. I followed around the tree and behind it and found a spot in the chain link fence that was missing a part of the fencing, creating a hole behind the tree. The giant oak tree obscured it from sight almost deliberately.

I heard the sound again and followed it through the fence into the forest. I remember feeling what I now know as anxious, but watching my own toddlers, I realize at that age we do not have any concept of fear. So, I didn't know at that time what I was feeling. Curiosity got the better of me and I continued to follow the sound down a path that led into the forest away from the property. Being August, it was still light out at the time so I could see where I was going, however, the light was beginning to fade at this point. I followed the direction of the sound. I cannot tell you what it sounded like, except it seemed to have drawn me closer to it. Almost in a trance like, although at the time I didn't fully understand that either. The sound kept pulling me, like it had tied a rope around my waist and was slowly pulling me towards its center. I remember wanting to run but couldn't. It pulled me until I no longer could see the path I was on.

I remember hearing my sister's voice calling my name, but I cannot remember if I answered or if I even acknowledged her efforts of trying to locate me. The pull of the sound entrapped me in a seemingly oblivious state of hypnotic gravitation. Being so young at the time I did not understand the danger I was in or the gravity of the situation. I do remember that the closer I got to the sound, the calmer I felt. I know, weird, right?

The closer I got to the sound, the louder it became as well. I compare the sound to that of a jet engine. Just deafening the closer you get to it. I came to a stop atop of a ravine, below it was a creek, moving swiftly along the bottom of it. I remember staring down at it, blankly, almost like I didn't know what it was I was seeing. As I stood there, I felt a small tug at my shirt, investigating what could have tugged at my shirt. I was flung down the ravine and went tumbling head over feet barreling towards the bottom. This must have snapped me out of whatever trance-like state I was in because I remember I began to scream and started clawing at the damp earth in effort to stop the tumbling. A root of a tree was jutting out of the earth creating a pocket between the ground and the root in which my arm found it and abruptly brought me to a stop just inches from the water. My feet dangling in the water as the current viciously lapped at them.

I was hurt, but at the time I could not tell you how bad. Later I found out I had broken my arm that was caught in the tree from the fall. At that time, I may have just been in shock, as I struggled to get my feet out of the water and my arm from its snare. I broke free of the root hold and was able to pull myself up onto a small boulder that was positioned on one side of me. Laying there I begin to cry, from the pain, but mainly from the fear that had abruptly set in. Crying loudly, I heard my sister call for me. Unsure as to if I were actually hearing her or just stunned from the fall, I stopped crying and listened. When I was sure I heard her, I screamed, and I kept screaming. I screamed until I saw her above me at the top of the ravine. She did not waste time, she slid on her butt all the way to me.

When she came to me, she hugged me and promised that she would get me out of the ravine. I remember her looking around for something and someplace flatter to crawl back out of the ravine. She helped me get to my feet and we began walking along the creek. Disturbing the quiet of the forest with the sloshing noise we made as we walked through the water.

We came to a makeshift bridge a little ways down the creek that connected the two sides of the ravine over the creek. She shimmied me up onto her shoulders and literally threw me onto the bridge. She told me to wait there, and she jumped up and drug herself onto the bridge. It was then she checked me over and discovered my arm was broken. She tore her shirt and made a sling from it to support my arm.

Standing me up she led from the bridge onto a small dirt path and into the forest. It was pitch black in the forest at this time, and despite it being August, the forest was chilly at night, both of us wet from the fall and the creek, we began to shiver. I remember her comforting me but did not recognize the anxiety in her voice as she realized we were lost in the woods. Not being familiar with an area and being dark, the forest will play tricks on your mind. We must have walked a mile or so before it started to rain. The thunder startled us both and my sister found a giant hole in a huge tree we could take shelter in. She held me close and sang me a lullaby to sleep.

I woke to my sister standing outside the hole of the tree, watching out into the forest. I struggled to scoot out of the hole to see what she was looking at. I called her name, but she didn't hear me. I called her name again and she turned to face me, she smiled and held out her hand. She helped me up and took my hand. We began walking along the path that was now visible with the morning light. She did not say a word the whole way out of the forest. She would just nod and smile at my incessant chattering.

Stopping every so often to stare back at the direction we had come from, back at the hole in the tree we had spent the night before huddled together in. We walked hand in hand down the path that I was on not twelve hours later. We walked the better part of the morning and looking back I do not remember the length of time it took us to walk into the forest. Time seemed to have slipped or all together stopped. I just simply cannot recall that part of this story.

The summer heat mixed with the rain the night before left the day sweltering and sticky. I remember telling her I was thirsty, and she squatted down in front of me, put her finger to my lips and told me to listen. It was the only thing she said to me. I stopped talking and listened, in the background I could faintly hear people yelling. What they were yelling, at first, I could not make out. She smiled and took my hand again and we started walking in the direction of the voices. The closer we got, the clearer the voices became. I then recognized them as the voices of our parents calling our names. As well as voices I did not recognize that were doing the same.

We continued to walk towards the sound of the voices until we came to a clearing in the forest that the sun was beaming through and met a crowd of people in a single file horizontal line calling our names. My mom was the first to spot us, followed by my dad and another man I now know was the Sheriff. My mom ran full speed at us and scooped me up in her arms. My sister smiled and let go of my hand. My dad closed in behind my mom and hugged us both from behind. She kissed me and sat me down to examine me. She noticed my arm tied in my sister's shirt and realized I was hurt. Looking around she asked, *"Where's your sister?"*

Confused by this statement I turned around to see my sister standing there, smiling and I told my mom, "What do you mean, she's right there?" and I pointed to where I saw her standing. My sister smiled at me, winked, and then she was gone. I remember standing there just dumbfounded. Utterly confused. But I knew what to do, I knew where to go. I can't explain it, I just grabbed my mom's hand and with all my four-year-old strength led my parents back to the hole in the tree where my sister's body lay.

You see, my sister was injured on her slide down the ravine to save me. A root that was broken had punctured her side and her lung. It was not a big wound and at the time it was suspected she was not in tremendous pain. She would have been working on pure adrenaline at this point in which kept her from feeling pain in an effort to rescue me. Her will, determination, and love she had for her brother kept her going until he was safe. When she found the natural, makeshift, lodging in the tree and safely tucked me in for the night my sister simply fell asleep listening to the sound of the rain and never woke up.

I believe what she was looking at when I woke up the next morning was her spirit guide that was there to lead her to her next destination, but she couldn't go, not yet, she had to fulfill her honor bound brother duty and get me safely home. I believe it was the same guide that helped me show my parents to her body tucked neatly away in that tree. As far as what it was that led me into the forest that day, I cannot say. I will say that I have not heard it since.

I now own the same house my parents bought. The same tree covers the same hole in the fence, and I still take that path with my toddler to the same hole in the tree some thirty-five years later, to lay flowers in remembrance of my sister's love. I installed a bench next to the tree, so that I can come and sit with her and feel her presence to this very day. I was four years old when my sister died, I do not remember much of that time frame, but I do remember that faith filled August day. A memory forever ingrained in my mind, reminding me of just how much of my sister's love I truly had.

Graphic art by Gwen Luckett (Reference "A Sister's Love")

THE TREE

Summers spent at my grandparents were anything but boring. There were five of us kids, so plenty of fun, plenty of noise and just enough grandparents that they could tag team if they needed to in order to wrangle five crazy kids in. I remember them all quite well, swimming in the makeshift swimming pool, swimming lessons at the local public pool, conning my granddad for another popsicle, racing his lawnmowers down the street, laughing at his angry antics when we do that. Just good memories to help drown out the bad. There was one summer in particular I don't think any of us will forget, I know I sure didn't.

I think I was about twelve years old, the youngest of the bunch so that meant the most gullible to do the betting of the others. We took a camping trip with my grandparents to a remote location known only by the hair on our chins, no GPS back then just road maps left to my grandparents fighting about the direction of it. We drove what seemed like hours, we started in the morning, and it was dusk by the time we finally came to our camp. I remember being taken by the wide-open space surrounded by green, luscious, huge trees. We all piled out of that rusty old station wagon, each of us carrying some sort of camping gear or another and as the older kids helped set up tents and collect firewood, I had the task of helping my grandmother set up for dinner and walked with her to collect water from a freshwater spring.

We walked through the trees on a path that had been cleared from years of trampling. There were human and animal tracks mingling in the dirt. I walked behind her, my eyes wandered around, mesmerized at the beauty and tranquility of the forest. I could hear all kinds of wildlife. Birds chirping and rustling in the trees, twigs cracking from chipmunks scurrying around, cricket chirping bringing in the night. She called back to me to stay close and not wander off the path. I quickly caught up to her and she turned and smiled at me as she walked on. I don't know how far away from the campsite we walked, I kept looking behind me at the glow of the clearing until it faded into trees and vines.

"Um, granny, are we lost?' I asked her

She turned and smiled at me, shook her head, and continued walking on. I ran up beside her and took her hand, she looked down at me, squeezed it and we walked on, hand in hand. It wasn't long after I could hear the whoosh of water running wildly and the freshwater spring came into view. I remember it being so clear I could see my reflection bounce back at me as if it were a mirror. I bent down and let the water run through my fingers. The chill of it was like ice running through my veins. I shivered and stood up, wiping my hands on my shorts.

"Cold, isn't it?" Granny said laughing as she took the bucket she had been carrying and dipped it in the water.

"Yeah, very!" I responded excitedly, laughing.

I too was carrying a bucket, granny said it was for washing the dishes, and I dipped it in the water shivering as the water hit my hands and splashed my arms. I watched the water rush in, colliding with the edges of the bucket, breaking around it and continuing downstream. I watched my reflection wrinkle in the ripples of the water and became hypnotized by the serenity of it. I watched my reflection distort and dance in the water so eloquently, cascading against the bucket, breaking and disappearing around it. Watching I did not notice the cold that took over my body, nor the numbness in my fingers. In a trance I must have set the bucket down and wandered into the stream deeper, fixed on the motion of the water guiding me into oblivion.

I watched the water and walked. I watched it until my reflection collided with that of a tree. A magnificent tree that its reflection seemed to take up the whole stream and then some. A reflection swallowed up mine like night swallows day. I followed the reflection with my eyes, through the water, up the embankment, and landed on the tree itself. It was standing there, seeming alone. Its vastness did not allow room for anything else. A beautifully monstrous tree. Its limbs reached even further in every direction. Most of which hung down and crawled along the bank of the stream and into the water as if it were drinking from it.

I stood there in the middle of the stream staring at this creature of the forest. I had never seen anything so majestic, so surreal. Tantalizing even. I did not notice everything going quiet around me, all I could hear was the water sloshing against my legs. I was so caught in the grasp of the tree's presence that I did not hear my grandmother calling my name, nor heard her frantically rushing in the water. I did not hear anything but that tree calling to me.

When she reached me, her rough firm grip on my arm made me flinch just a little, but I still did not look away from this tree. She swung me around and shook me violently, but I still did not answer. It was not until she slapped me across my face that I blinked and looked at her confused as to why she had hit me and why I was standing waist deep in the water. She cupped my face and looked sternly into my eyes, and spoke," You must never cross this stream, you hear me, never. Stay out of the water and on that side of. Promise me!"

I looked at her still confused, she shook me again and screamed, 'PROMISE ME!'
I did and she took my hands and led me back to the side we were on. The tree still running through my mind that I did not hear her talking to me the rest of the way back to camp, the rest of the night was just a blur. That night I dreamt of the tree, it called to me in my sleep. Called to me to come back to the water, its limbs reaching out to me caressing my face and body before they wrapped around my neck and waist and started pulling me. I fought violently to get away and could not, I fought so hard I hit my cousin square in the face causing her to wake up.
"Max, hey, Max! Wake up, wake up, it's only a dream, Max!" she called to me
I woke to her holding me by my shoulders and looking at me pale as can be and a bright red welt on her face where I hit her.

Horrified, I apologized intently, she smiled, gave me a hug and laid down next to me. I did not sleep the rest of the night. I laid awake afraid to sleep, afraid that if I did, I would not wake up. The next morning, we all decided to go to the lake that was adjacent to the campground and swim. It was 6:00 am and already pushing 90. We all had breakfast and gathered up our towels and headed to the lake. The others ran ahead of me and my grandparents, yelling and carrying on as they rushed towards the lake. My grandparents laughed and looked back at me.
"Do you not want to go swimming Max?" My granddad asked

I looked up at him and gave a sheepish smile and replied, "Yes, I am just tired, I had a nightmare and couldn't sleep."
"Oh? You want to talk about it?' he asked
"Not really." I responded and I walked ahead of them to catch up to the others.

When I reached them, the boys were already deep in the water, splashing and carrying on dunking each other. My cousin had spread out her towel in a sunny spot and was sitting on it, sunglasses on, rubbing tanning lotion on her skin. She looked up at me and smiled as I walked over to her and plopped down on the ground.
"You, ok?" she asked. I nodded and stared out at the water watching the boys attempt to play three-man chicken. I watched them awhile before I got up and spread my own towel out beside her and laid down next to her looking up at the sky and watched the clouds slowly drift by. My thoughts drifted back to the tree. I watched the clouds a little longer before I sighed loudly and rolled over to face my cousin.
"I saw something yesterday when granny and I went for water." I began

My cousin raised her head, pushed her sunglasses down the bridge of her nose and looked at me curiously. She rolled over and asked, "Is that what caused your nightmare?"
I rolled back onto my back, sighed heavily again and shakily said," I think so, I...I don't know exactly."
"Well tell me what you do know." she said
"I can't, I mean I don't know the words to say to even begin to tell you." I responded.
I sat up and brought my knees to my chest, hugging them. I began to cry. She sat up and hugged me and I cried harder. I do not know what I was crying about, I just had an overwhelming urge to do so. I lowered my knees and wiped my face, turning to her with swollen eyes. I told her I wanted to show her something, but that it had to be a secret. She pinkie swore and convinced our grandparents to let us explore the nearby woods under the cover of picking berries.

We walked back along the trail towards the campground, traded out flip flops for Keds and I led her towards the trail Granny and I walked the day before. I stopped at the entrance and looked back at my cousin. She smiled a sheepish smile and held out her hand as to say lead the way and I hesitantly walked into the forest with my cousin close behind. The summer heat dissipated the deeper we got into the forest. The trees provided a soothing coolness of shade. There was a slight breeze to circulate that coolness around us. We walked in silence. A tidbit I remember because the day before the forest was anything but silent. There was no rustling of birds or scurrying of small wildlife, there was only the sound of our feet crunching the ground beneath us and our breathing as we walked towards the freshwater stream.

I stopped short of the water's edge, hesitant to go any further. I stared across the water and fixed my eyes on the monstrous wonder, thinking for a second, it called my name. My cousin came up behind me asking what it was I wanted her to see. I just pointed across the way, my eyes never leaving the trees. She moved curiously around me and followed my stare and point. She looked back at me, confusion and intrigue ran across her face. She stepped closer to the water's edge, and I reached out to grab her arm. She protested slightly and stepped into the icy clear water. I protested even more, leery to step any further. I called out her name, but she seemed to have not heard me. Cautiously I followed behind her, not wanting her to get any closer to the tree, but we did.

I reached her and took her hand, she looked at me sternly and then down at my hand. I squeezed hers tightly and she returned the gesture. Grateful she was not lost in the enchantment of the tree, we walked hand in hand deeper into the crystal-clear water. We watched the water and followed the reflection of the tree. I kept looking from the water to the tree and back again, careful to watch where I was going. The sunlight would peek through openings in the trees as we approached closer, glistening off the water creating a bright spot in the water that made us squint against its magnificent glow. The tree seemed to reach for the bright spots, its limbs that kissed the edge of the water slowly creeping towards the light. We stopped when we noticed the movement of the limbs and watched in curious horror as the limbs dipped into the water and slowly snaked towards us. I squeezed her hand tighter. She looked at me with amazement and nodded her head towards the tree. I once again protested. She smiled and said, "Max, there is nothing here to be afraid of, do you not hear it?"

Confused, I looked back at the tree and closed my eyes. I felt the breeze dance my hair around my face and the water kiss gently against my legs. I breathed in the cool, damp air, let it fill my lungs, and listened. It was a faint whisper, barely even audible to my ears. I tried to focus on the sound. It was like tiny little bees buzzing in my ears. I took another deep breath in and concentrated. Quieting everything around me, I heard it, a smooth, silky voice gently graced my ears. So clear, yet so silent. I felt a wave of calm seep into my veins, a sensual tranquility I have yet to feel to this day. I wanted to run, every ounce of me tried to fight it, yet my feet would not move. I felt myself sinking deeper into the smooth sandy bottom of the stream. I did not realize my cousin let go of my hand, nor did I notice her walking towards the tree. I stood there, hypnotized by the calming, seductive voice in my ear consuming my entire being. I watched her move closer to the tree but was unable to speak or move. I was grounded in the water as I was a part of it. Unaware the tree's limbs were coiling around my torso, gently stroking my body and winding slowly up my torso and around my neck.

I felt a sting in the left side of my neck and suddenly a white hot sensation coursed through my veins. Sending excruciating pain throughout my body. I screamed out and began to struggle under the weight of the tree's limbs that were wrapped around me. Each time I moved, they tightened around me, suffocatingly. I screamed louder, I called for my cousin to help, I struggled thrashed against the water and the limbs. Each time the limbs got tighter and tighter, winding more and more around me. I felt a pull at my feet and horror flooded my soul as the limbs swiftly drug me under water. I tried desperately to get loose from its grasp, water filling my lungs, burning them. I felt the feeling go out of my feet first as it crept up my legs and soared through my body and I watched in horror as the crystal-clear water turned black around me.

I woke up on the embankment, coughing and spewing water and blood onto the ground, water dripping from every inch of me. I rolled over on my back and looked up to darkness. I shot straight up and called for my cousin. I scrambled to my feet in a frantic hysteria screaming her name. Something grabbed my arms, and I began to fight, violently, screaming.

"Shh, shhh, whoa, Max! You're ok, you're ok settle down now, you're ok!" I heard my grandmother say. I looked up at her in astonished bewilderment and fell into her arms and began to sob relentlessly. She held me there silently stroking my hair as my wet body soaked her clothes as well.

"There, there, now, let it all out." She said as she stroked my hair and back.

I wiped my face on her shirt and pushed back against her suddenly remembering my cousin.

"CARMEN! WHERE'S CARMEN!?" I yelled at her.

My granny took a deep breath and let go of me, wrapped a blanket she retrieved from the ground around me and sat me down again. She walked over to the water's edge and looked out into nothing. She wrapped her arms around her chest and just stood there. I got up and secured the blanket around me and walked over to where she was standing. She took a long deep breath in and let it out. She stood there a moment longer before speaking, never taking her eyes off the tree across the way. "Your mama thought this trip would help you, she thought if I brought you out here you would finally be able to move on from what happened."

Confused, I did not speak. I was trying to make sense of what she was telling me.

"Move on from what?" I asked her

"From the accident, Max, do you not remember?' She asked softly, almost reluctantly.

"Remember wha…?" I started to ask as the memories started to flood my head. Knocking me back.

"Oh my goodness, I..I forgot!" I exclaimed as I tried to run, she grabbed my arm.

"No sweetheart you didn't, that is why we are here. Do you not remember how you got here?' She asked as she took me by my shoulders and tried to pull me closer to her and the water. I struggled against her arms, refusing to come closer to her.

"MAX! Come, look, MAX! LOOK!" She exclaimed as she shoved me out in front of her and spun me around.

I didn't want to look; I didn't want to see that damn tree. She shook me violently and yelled, "LOOK DAMN IT, YOU NEED TO OPEN YOUR EYES AND LOOK!"

I lowered my head and slowly looked up. Following the water's ripples until it landed on the tree's reflection and followed the reflection up to the tree where I saw her. Horrified, I yelled," NO! CARMEN!' tears swallowed my eyes, and I began to shake. My knees buckled and I collapsed. My grandmother caught me and helped me stand. I closed my eyes again as my grandmother wrapped her arms around me from behind and pulled me to my feet. She whispered that it was ok and to look again. I shook my head and she whispered again more sternly," You Must!"

I swallowed hard and slowly opened my eyes and looked at the tree again, confusion sat in as I looked at a lone tree standing magnificently on the water's edge. I watched it with intention, studying it, waiting for it to move. Its only movement were its leaves against the breeze. I watched as memories flooded my mind again. My grandmother stood behind still holding on to me as I looked at the tree, I remembered. I remembered the summer I was 12 when my cousin, brothers, and I were camping with my grandparents. I remember the sounds and the smells. I remember my brothers and my cousin playing in the lake and then I remembered Carmen. I remembered Carmen, quiet, stoic, and not her usual chipper self.

I remember her wanting me to take a walk with her to the river and I remembered her walking us both out into the middle, I remember her telling me to not be afraid, letting go of my hand and watching her walk to the other side, stand beside the beautiful willow tree, and then I remembered the gunshot. It echoed so loud that everything went silent. I remember stumbling back, getting hung on a tree root in the water and falling, hitting my head on a rock and losing consciousness.

I fell to the ground sobbing uncontrollably, I remembered everything. My grandmother went down with me, still holding me, rocking me back and forth. That summer I never forgot, but my brain set aside the memories that haunted me for ten years. Plaquing my dreams both day and night. Causing my parents to put me into a hospital as I ranted about a monstrously beautiful tree that came to life and tried to kill me. Never able to comprehend the horrific trauma I witnessed. Never able to cope with the suicide of my dearest cousin, not until I was 22 years old, and I went camping with my grandparents one last time.

Photo by Rachael Hinkley

Author Biography

Oklahoma native and wife of a 22-year Army Veteran. A mother of three crazy boys and bonus mother to an amazing, beautiful girl and one more wacky boy. Two fur babies as well as a fur grandbaby and a yes, one more crazy grandson. Spent my days wrestling boys into submission by myself and produced a United States Marine, an upcoming musician and producer, and an aspiring cook and gamer. I loved writing as a child and young adult and had to put it on hold for life. A talented dental assistant by trade.

I decided to spread my wings and explore the world and travel as much as I can. Fiery personality and a heart as big as Texas, writing came second nature to me, never giving it up, just pocketed it until I had the courage to set it free. I love being at the beach and anything outdoors. I have been described as crafty, thrifty, and sarcastic. I love a challenge and have welcomed this new chapter in my life with grace and honor.

Made in the USA
Columbia, SC
08 October 2024